TRANSFORMATIONAL
THOUGHTS

A Journey to Becoming Fully Transformed

DABO H. DAVIES

Copyright 2020, Dabo Davies

All rights reserved. This book or any portion thereof may not be reproduced or used in any manner whatsoever without the express written permission of the publisher.

PRINTED IN UNITED KINGDOM **ISBN:** 9798651441488

DH DAVIES GLOBAL LONDON
UNITED KINGDOM

WWW.DHDAVIES.ORG

APPRECIATION

All that I know is a total of what I have been taught, first, by the Holy Spirit, and from all those who have taught me in my journey, both directly and indirectly.

I am forever grateful to the countless exceptional people who, by their commitment and devotion to becoming the best they could be, have inspired me to do the same.

I am ever mindful of the unmatched love, prayer, support, and patience of my precious wife, Elizabeth.

To my countless partners worldwide who through their love and passion have shown kindness and support, I say THANK YOU!

DEDICATION

To anyone reading this book, in whom is the potential of living a fully transformed life.

TABLE OF CONTENTS

APPRECIATION iii

DEDICATION v

TABLE OF CONTENTS vii

1   PERSONAL DEVELOPMENT 1

    1.1 Day 1: Self-Worth 2
        1.1.1   Importance of understanding your self-worth................. 5
        1.1.2   Think and Act 5
    1.2 Day 2: One Thing 9
        1.2.1   Think and Act 11
    1.3 Day 3: Be Teachable... 15
        1.3.1   Qualities of teachable persons 17
        1.3.2   Think and Act 18
    1.4 Day 4: Be Definitive... 21
        1.4.1   Think and Act 25
    1.5 Day 5: Little... 29
        1.5.1   Think and Act 31
    1.6 Day 6: More... 34
        1.6.1   Think and Act 36
    1.7 Day 7: Silence.. 39
        1.7.1   Think and Act 41
    1.8 Day 8: Privacy Settings.. 44
        1.8.1   Think and Act 46

1.9	Day 9: Leverage	49
	1.9.1　Some practical examples	50
	1.9.2　Think and Act	51

2　PERSONAL EFFECTIVENESS 55

2.1	Day 10: Vision	56
	2.2.1　Think and Act	58
2.2	Day 11: Planning	61
	2.2.1　Think and Act	63
2.3	Day 12: Break Records	66
	2.3.1　Think and Act	68
2.4	Day 13: Do	71
	2.4.1　Think and Act	74
2.5	Day 14: Problem-solving	78
	2.5.1　Think and Act	80
2.6	Day 15: Intentional	84
	2.6.1　Think and Act	86
2.7	Day 16: Questions	89
	2.7.1　Think and Act	92
2.8	Day 17: Insist	95
	2.8.1　Think and Act	97

3　FORGING AHEAD 101

3.1	Day 18: Obstacles	102
	3.1.1　Think and Act	104
3.2	Day 19: Through	107
	3.2.1　Think and act	110
3.3	Day 20: Fear	113
	3.3.1　Think and Act	115

- 3.4 Day 21: The Beautiful Pain 118
  - *3.4.1 Think and Act* *120*
- 3.5 Day 22: Continue 124
  - *3.5.1 Think and Act* *126*
- 3.6 Day 23: Decisions 129
  - *3.6.1 Think and Act* *132*
- 3.7 Day 24: Precision 135
  - *3.7.1 Think and Act* *137*
- 3.8 Day 25: Expectations 140
  - *3.8.1 Think and Act* *142*
- 3.9 Day 26: Concentration 145
  - *3.9.1 Think and Act* *147*

4 GO FOR IT! 151

- 4.1 Day 27: Create 152
  - *4.1.1 Think and Act* *154*
- 4.2 Day 28: No Middle Ground 157
  - *4.2.1 Think and Act* *159*
- 4.3 Day 29: Don't Quit 162
  - *4.3.1 Think and Act* *164*
- 4.4 Day 30: Wise Counsel 167
  - *4.4.1 Think and Act* *169*
- 4.5 Day 31: Personal Action 172
  - *4.5.1 Think and Act* *174*
- 4.6 Day 32: Goodbye 177
  - *4.6.1 Think and Act* *179*

PERSONAL DEVELOPMENT

There are two kinds of people – those who leave everything to chance and those who take deliberate steps to shape their destiny. If you want to be successful in your career, business, or any other sphere of life, you will need to take some proactive steps that will set you up for success.

Successful people understand that success only comes to those who actively work towards achieving just that. It might be true that opportunity knocks once on everyone's door but if you are not prepared, you might squander the opportunity. Personal development is the surest way of getting ready for the next time opportunity comes knocking and when opportunity meets your prepared, success will be inevitable. In this section, we delve into some transformational thoughts that can help you to become the best version of yourself.

1.1 Day 1: Self-Worth

**My Transformational Thought for today is:
'Self-Worth'**

The dictionary defines self-worth as "the sense of one's value or worth as a person."

Expert psychologists believe that self-worth should be less about measuring yourself based on external actions and more about valuing your inherent worth as a person. In other words, self-worth is about who you are, not about what you do.

This means it really doesn't matter what you do, what you own, or where you live - if your perception of who you are is worthless, it will strongly affect not only you but also how you interact with others. You may not like this, but there is always someone who looks more attractive than you, someone who is richer than you, and maybe someone who appears successful than you. However high you get in life, there will always be someone that seems higher.

The worst thing you can do is define success based on what other people have. Don't think of success as a comparison because the only person you should be competing with is yourself.

Dr. Myles Munroe's approach in defining success is worth paying attention to, he said;

> *"Success is not making a lot of money; it's not having a big house or a car, success is not having a lot of friends. Success is the completion and the successful fulfilment of the original intent or purpose for your existence or why something was made. SUCCESS IS YOU DISCOVERING YOUR PURPOSE AND COMPLETING IT BEFORE YOU DIE. Success is not measured by what you have done compared to what others have done. Success is measured by what you have done compared to what you should and could have done. Success is measured by what you can do, success must be measured by why you have been created; Therefore, the only person who knows how successful you are is you and God. It's possible to be successful in a wrong assignment, so, the key to success is ASSIGNMENT or purpose, and the purpose must come from your manufacturer. The key to your success is your original purpose in God's plan for humanity. You were created with purpose and for a purpose"*

Unfortunately, this is not how society views success. Society tells us that to feel successful, we need to be better than other people. Even in the corporate world, awards are usually given to top employees based on some form of competition. This introduces the problem of measuring ourselves with others, rather than focusing on identifying, developing, and maximizing our inherent value. The Bible is the greatest manual on self-worth so, let's have a look at what it has to say on the subject.

> *"Oh, don't worry; we wouldn't dare say that we are as wonderful as these other men who tell you how important they are! But they are only comparing themselves with each other, using themselves as the standard of measurement. How ignorant!"*
>
> **(2 Corinthians 10:12, New Living Translation).**

In this scripture, it is clear that the Apostle Paul knew his worth. Unlike some of his contemporaries who were comparing themselves with each other, he focused on his purpose because he knew he was uniquely different. He knew he didn't have to have the same kind of results with the other Apostles because they all had different callings. His final analysis was that the reason they were comparing themselves with each other was that they were ignorant.

The same can be said of anyone that tries to peg their self-worth on public opinion. Constantly comparing yourself to others is like fighting a lost battle because it really won't matter whether or not you outperform the other persons; your defeat is already displayed in your comparison

Self-Worth

Chili pepper in tomato stew analogy:

The chili pepper in a tomato stew anecdote was given by a man who had eaten chili pepper his entire life. Chili pepper doesn't have to get worked up by the fact that the cook just added lots of tomatoes to the stew. It doesn't matter how many tomatoes are added because just a little bit of chili pepper in the dish will leave an unignorable taste that no amount of tomatoes could ever achieve. This analogy underscores the importance of self-worth. Just like the chili pepper, you should always know that your contribution makes a huge difference – even if it doesn't look like it does.

1.1.1 Importance of understanding your self-worth

- It increases your confidence
- It eliminates competition
- It creates room for proper application of your skill
- It increases dependency on your skill
- It gives you inner peace
- It helps you to celebrate your accomplishments

1.1.2 Think and Act

We many times accomplish things and never acknowledge our successes, achievements, and our skills and talents. Why not take a moment today, identify something you accomplished that brought joy to you, and celebrate it, and I mean to celebrate it?

Personal Development

Take the following self-assessment quiz.

a) What activities make you feel good about yourself?

b) What positive habits can You develop to improve your self-worth?

c) Do you feel comfortable in your skin?

d) What have you done lately that reveals who you are?

e) What have you done lately that makes you feel very happy within? It may be something as insignificant to you as joining a dance class.

f) Can you identify people who encourage you, and surround yourself with them? You can start with just one person.

g) Can you identify an inspirational person who has overcome their self-worth issues? Someone you know, someone in the bible, or maybe someone you have read about.

NOTES

_____

_____

_____

_____

_____

_____

Self-Worth

NOTES

NOTES

1.2 Day 2: One Thing

My Transformational Thought today is:
'ONE THING'

Everyone has at least ONE THING. And that is all that matters. You do not need very many things to make it in life – you just need one thing.

Successful people have mastered the art of single-tasking. Facebook's founder, Mark Zuckerberg has always been a coder – just like Google's Larry Page or Microsoft's Bill Gates. Peter Theil, the founder of PayPal has always been a hedge fund manager even before he founded PayPal. Howard Schultz of Starbucks is a marketing genius just like Steve Jobs was. The list could go on and on but the bottom line is, every successful person found their "one thing" and stuck with it. Their one thing has made them a household name.

If the most successful people in the world have attained success by discovering their one thing, it would be a wise move to follow suit. And the best part is everyone has their "one thing" and all you have is to discover it. Just ask yourself this - what's the one thing you can bring to the table in such a way that many lives will be transformed?

The one thing you have in your possession becomes increasingly minute and insignificant as long as you keep your focus on what others have or are engaged in. But if you focus on your one thing, you might be pleasantly surprised at how much you have to offer. Even if it seems like there isn't much going for you, discovering your one thing might place you on the global map.

The Psalmist had an interesting prayer;

> *One thing I ask from the LORD, this only do I seek: that I may dwell in the house of the LORD all the days of my life, to gaze on the beauty of the LORD and to seek him in his temple.*
> **(Psalms 27:4, New International Version)**

David understood the power of focusing on one thing. As a result, he went down in history as one of the greatest Psalmists that has ever lived. That was his one thing. And the musicians of our day borrow heavily from his Psalms when writing their music. He not only discovered his one thing but he is now helping many others to discover theirs. Discovering your one thing is not just about achieving personal success but also about helping others to discover their purpose. In other words, when you discover your one thing, it might help others discover their one thing as well.

By the time you finish reading this, someone will have leveraged the power of Facebook and Instagram to launch a worldwide e-commerce business with little or no capital. That serves to show how there are opportunities all around you. Unfortunately, you won't recognize or seize these opportunities until you discover your one thing. Most people neglect or despise their one thing because it appears too small or insignificant. But everything you admire today was once just an idea. Rome was built but not in a day. You must be willing to take a step of faith and unleash your one thing. Do not allow the fear of failure to cripple you. You lose 100% of the shots you don't take. Just put yourself out there and see what happens!

You may want to stop looking for SOMETHING and just focus on that ONE THING.

 1.2.1   Think and Act

Think of some ways in which your indecision or decision not to unleash your one thing might have deprived others of the opportunity to identify their one thing.

Personal Development

Take the following self-assessment quiz;

a) Have you identified your ONE THING?

b) Identify the factors that might be limiting you from identifying your ONE THING

c) Have you encountered any setbacks in unleashing your ONE THING?

d) Do you need help in developing your ONE THING?

NOTES

NOTES

NOTES

1.3 Day 3: Be Teachable

**My Transformational Thought today is:
'Be Teachable'**

The dictionary describes a teachable individual as one who is capable of being taught or instructed. Children are naturally curios and willing to learn new things. Just think of all the crazy things you believed when you were a toddler just because mommy or daddy said so. But as we grow older, we tend to be less trusting and as such, we start to lose our natural ability to accept new information. This could be a good thing because there is a lot of misinformation in the world – but it could also be bad if you completely block out all new information.

Personal Development

The great motivational speaker Zig Ziglar put it this way;

> 'If you are not WILLING to LEARN, no one can help you, but if you are DETERMINED to LEARN, no one can stop you'

See, learning is a choice – and so is ignorance. Being teachable will require you to get out of your comfort zone because it is seldom easy. But the results of being teachable will make the experience worth it.

In this digital era, the knowledge economy is the most important section of the economy. And knowledge is not to be confused with education. Even if you are highly educated, you still need to have a teachable heart. Each new day, new inventions and discoveries keep emerging. What was considered as factual a couple of years ago may no longer be so because of some new information? Even some of Einstein's theories are being revised by modern physicists. For instance, scientists have reportedly discovered an atom that travels faster than light.

We live in a very dynamic world and the only constant thing in this generation is change. Bob Proctor aptly said;

> "The illiterate of the 21st century will not be those who can't read or write, but those who are unwilling to learn, unlearn, and relearn."

It is not just enough to learn. You must also be ready to unlearn what you learned whenever new information comes up, for only then can you learn new things. The greatest hindrance to the acquisition of new knowledge is old knowledge. Old knowledge is great but only as long as it is not outdated. That is why organizations spend millions of dollars on refresher courses for their staff.

No one wants to have to deal with someone that is not teachable – whether in the market place or social settings, being teachable makes you more likable which ultimately helps you to cultivate and maintain more rewarding relationships.

> *'For whoever has a teachable heart, to him, more understanding will be given; and whoever does not have a yearning for truth, even what he has will be taken away from him."*
>
> **(Mark 4:25, Amplifies Bible).**

Those who are not teachable end up stuck in the past while the world swiftly flies past them into the future. If you want to remain on the cutting edge in your industry, you must have a teachable spirit.

1.3.1 Qualities of teachable persons

So, how do you know whether or not you are teachable? Well, there are a couple of qualities that every teachable person has. The following are some of these qualities.

- They are self-effacing
- They listen well
- They acknowledge their errors and fix them
- They continually seek more knowledge
- They surround themselves with seasoned educators.

Teachable people are often rewarded by accolades, promotions, and high achievement. To put it simply, it PAYS to be teachable.

Personal Development

 1.3.2   Think and Act

Would you say that you are a teachable person? If not, what can you do to improve? If yes, how has that helped you in your career/business?

Take the following self-assessment quiz;

- a) Are you willing to learn?
- b) How teachable are you?
- c) Think of a situation in which you demonstrated your willingness to learn
- d) Think of a situation in which your unwillingness to learn cost you something
- e) What are the 5 qualities of a teachable person as identified in this section?

NOTES

_____

_____

_____

_____

_____

_____

_____

NOTES

NOTES

1.4   Day 4: Be Definitive

My Transformational Thought today is:
'BE DEFINITE'

The dictionary defines the word 'DEFINITE' as:- clearly defined or determined; not vague or general; fixed; precise; exact:

The sun is the source of all energy on earth. Apart from the solar energy that we get from the sun, sunlight can also be used to produce electricity through photovoltaic cells. The sun also heats the earth's surface and then the earth's surface provides heat for the atmosphere thereby causing wind which can be harnessed for wind energy. Both flora and fauna also rely on energy from the sun for various biological functions. But as powerful as the sun is, you wouldn't get scorched by it.

How come the biggest source of energy doesn't cause us serious harm? Well, it's because the sun rays that reach us don't focus. If you took a lens and used it to focus the sun rays, you can easily convert the otherwise harmless rays into heat energy – the kind that can start a fire in a couple of seconds. That is the power of focus. There is an interesting statement in scripture that illustrates this truth. Here it is;

> "That I may receive my sight"

I have taken the time to study this statement and I just love it. This statement shows a definite request from a man who literally could not see. As you may imagine, he probably had a million other needs but when he met Christ, he focused on one – he was DEFINITE.

> "And Jesus said, "What do you want Me to do for you?" The blind man said to Him, "Rabboni (my Master), let me regain my sight." Jesus said to him, "Go; your faith [and confident trust in My power] has made you well." Immediately he regained his sight and began following Jesus on the road."
>
> **[MARK 10:51-52, Amplified Bible]**

Notice how the question presented to him was OPEN, and then notice the precision in his response. He had an exact request - his goal was clearly defined and fixed.

Just like this blind man, you must form a clear mental picture of the things you want, and DO with faith and purpose all that can be done each day in achieving it. You must be definite in your goals for only then can you realize the fruition of your dreams.

Being definite emphasizes the strength of your opinion and belief. A definite decision or opinion is firm and clear, and unlikely to be changed. Even when the going gets tough, you still stick to your goals because when the going gets tough, the tough get going.

The ability to fix your thought on a particular thing has the power to cause it to be created. Your mind is more powerful than you think. Start fixating on what you want and before you know it, you will get it. This is how a positive mental attitude works – you stay positive and continue believing in your dreams and before you know it, your dreams start manifesting right before your eyes.

A definite person behaves or talks in a firm, confident way. Check out what Jesus says in this regard:

> *"I assure you and most solemnly say to you, whoever says to THIS MOUNTAIN, 'Be lifted up and thrown into the SEA!' and does not doubt in his heart [in God's unlimited power], but BELIEVES that what he says is going to take place, it will be done for him [in accordance with God's will]."*
>
> **[MARK 11:23 Amplified Bible]**

It takes a person who is definite to look at a mountain and command it to vanish. And no, it doesn't have to be a physical mountain. There are many insurmountable hurdles on the path of anyone trying to achieve anything meaningful in life. You can look at these hurdles and throw in the towel, or you can approach them with confidence and faith that they will dissipate right before your eyes.

Napoleon Hill also taught the importance of definitiveness in planning. He said;

> "Create a DEFINITE plan for carrying out your desire and begin at once, whether you are ready or not, to put this plan into action."

Some might argue that it is better to get ready before you start executing your plan. The reality however is if the plan is definite, you can start executing it right away. A definite plan is similar to what is often referred to as a **SMART** goal. It is a plan that is **Specific, Measurable, Attainable, Realistic, and Timebound.**

This reminds me of the time I was taking my 7-year-old to school. As we started discussing his expectations, I gave him a quote that I had heard before, and as little as he is, he was able to streamline his goal to something specific. He wants to play football, and was also precise on what position he feels he has the potential to be the best at;

> "Keep your mind fixed on what you want in life: not on what you don't want."

Through my interactions with people, I have realized that most people know precisely what they don't want. As a consequence, they tend to focus their energies on what they do not want instead of focusing their energies on what they want. They spend a lot of time trying to prevent or avoid what they do not want instead of preparing, planning, and working for what they want.

Being definite does not negate the fact that there will be challenges, setbacks, or delays, but your mind must be fixed on the goal. The story of Abraham gives us a clear example. Here is what the scriptures say;

> *"In hope against hope Abraham believed that he would become a FATHER OF MANY NATIONS, as he had been promised [by God]: "SO [numberless] SHALL YOUR DESCENDANTS BE." Without becoming weak in faith, he considered his own body, now as good as dead [for producing children] since he was about a hundred years old, and [he considered] the deadness of Sarah's womb. BUT HE DID NOT DOUBT or WAVER in unbelief concerning the promise of God, but he grew strong and empowered by faith, giving glory to God, being fully convinced that God had the power to do what He had promised."*
>
> **[ROMANS 4:18-21 Amplified Bible]**

6 things to learn about Abraham.

- He acknowledged the challenge (his body as good as dead and the deadness of Sarah's womb)
- His mind was FIXED
- He NEVER doubted nor wavered
- He was GRATEFUL
- He was CONVINCED
- He RECEIVED the promise

1.4.1 Think and Act

a) What do you want in life?
b) Are you convinced about it?
c) How can you achieve it?

d) What are the possibilities of achieving it?
e) Have you created a mental picture of it?
f) Have you placed it in a position where your mind will constantly be reminded of it?
g) Are you already grateful for it?
h) What are the potential challenges?

Don't lose your DEFINITE because of the available probable.

Think and Act

NOTES

NOTES

Personal Development

NOTES

1.5　Day 5: Little

My Transformational Thought today is:
'LITTLE'

I received this during a late-night strategic meeting:

The dictionary defines the word 'LITTLE' as:

a) small in consideration, importance, position, affluence

b) Not very important or serious

c) Something not BIG, or not MUCH.

We often downplay the little we have without realizing that therein lies the secret to much. Faithfulness is demonstrated in little. And once you have proved faithful in the little, you can then be entrusted with much. This is what the great teacher, Jesus, taught. Here is what he said;

> *"The one who manages the little he has been given with faithfulness and integrity will be promoted and trusted with greater responsibilities. But those who cheat with the little they have been given will not be considered trustworthy to receive more."*
>
> **(Luke 16:10 The Passion Translation)**

Most people make the expensive mistake of thinking that they will only take things seriously once they have something big to manage. But it doesn't work that way. You've got to start where you are with what you have. There is an African proverb that says, "you cannot climb a tree from the branches." Everything you admire today had to begin small.

Before you were born, you were a fetus in your mother's womb. Before you become a fetus, you were an embryo. And before you became an embryo, you were just a zygote. But look at you today- a fully grown human being. That is how life is fashioned. Everything begins small and then gradually grows to become huge. You should never despise any small responsibility you are given – it is just but a stepping stone to something greater. But the only way to get promoted to the next level is if you prove to be faithful in your little.

Martin Luther King will always be remembered for his inspirational words. One of his famous quotes is;

> *"If a man is called to be a street sweeper, he should sweep streets even as a Michelangelo painted, or Beethoven composed music or*

> *Shakespeare wrote poetry. He should sweep streets so well that all the hosts of heaven and earth will pause to say, 'Here lived a great street sweeper who did his job well."*

Do not waste your days wishing you had something else to do. Do not waste your years wishing you were someone else. The sad reality is that even the people you admire in life are probably not living a fulfilled life. Instead of focusing on the big things you lack, start focusing on the little you have. it is in those little things that you will truly find your happiness and fulfillment in life.

What you consider big today might be small tomorrow. And what you consider small today might be big tomorrow. So just live one day at a time with the determination to make your little as big as possible. Treat your little with reverence and with passion. Remember, you will not get promoted to the next level in life until you pass the test of being faithful in the little that you have been entrusted with at your current stage.

1.5.1   Think and Act

a) What are you doing with what you have?

b) It's okay to identify what you have is not enough, but what are you doing with that 'NOT ENOUGH'? - this also applies to time, access, opportunities, space, resources, people, etc.

NOTES

NOTES

1.6 Day 6: More

My Transformational Thought today is:
'MORE'

MORE can be defined as:

a) Something in greater quantity, amount, measure, degree, or number

b) something of greater importance

c) It is used to emphasize the large size of something

There is often a misconception that wanting more is a sign of greed. While all greedy people are always looking for more, not all people who want more are greedy. Everyone must always desire to have more. The desire for more demonstrates your belief in continuous improvement.

The Japanese have an interesting business philosophy called Kaizen. Kaizen means, "continuous improvement." They believe in always staying ahead of their competition by bettering their best. That is the right way of looking at the concept of more. It's not about greed but continuous improvement.

When you stop desiring more, you stagnate and that can be dangerous. When runoff water stagnates in a pond, it will start to stink in no time. But if water keeps running in the river, it stays fresh. The same can be said of us. Stagnation in life makes you less productive in almost all areas of your life. And the best way to avoid reaching here is to always desire more.

It is ABNORMAL not to desire to live MORE abundantly. Jesus believed that his followers should always desire more in life and that explains why he said,

> *"The thief cometh not, but for to steal, and to kill, and to destroy: I am come that they might have life, and that they might have it MORE abundantly."*
>
> **(John 10:10 King James Version)**

Abundant life" is a term used to refer to the fullness of life. And this should be the expectation of everyone.

This kind of life may include expectations of prosperity and health, but may also include other forms of fullness of life when faced with adverse circumstances.

The term "abundant life" refers to having a superabundance of a thing. It refers to life in its abounding fullness of joy and strength for MIND, BODY, and SOUL. It signifies a contrast to feelings of lack, emptiness, and dissatisfaction, and such feelings may motivate every sensible individual to seek for the meaning of life and a change in their life.

We need to highlight this thought on MORE (Abundant Life) because many equate poverty with spirituality and sickness with God's discipline and punishment. But that is just falsehood. Spirituality has nothing to do with poverty or sickness. You can still be pious and prosperous.

Wanting MORE, getting MORE, and being MORE is nothing to be ashamed of, but simply how things are meant to be in our universe. Wanting more means, you attain wholesome prosperity that encompasses a prosperous mind, a prosperous body, and a prosperous soul. In the words of scripture,

> *"Beloved, I pray that in EVERY WAY you may succeed and prosper and be in good health [physically], just as I know your soul prospers [spiritually]."*
>
> **(3 JOHN 1:2 Amplified Bible)**

1.6.1 Think and Act

a) What part of these 3 areas (Mind, Body, Soul) are you ignoring?

b) Do you realize that there is an imbalance if you are not abounding in these 3 areas (spirit soul and body)?

c) What steps can you take to ensuring you are 'having life MORE abundantly'?

More

NOTES

Personal Development

NOTES

1.7　Day 7: Silence

My Transformational Thought for today:
'SILENCE'

Silence in this context is a state of refraining oneself from speaking.

Most times the best and wisest words are illustrated by SILENCE. A fool will always speak because they have to say something but a wise person only speaks because they have something to say. Sometimes, it pays to just keep silent. The Chinese have a proverb that goes, "even the fish would not be caught by the fisherman if he only kept his mouth shut." Solomon, the wise man, had a lot to say on this topic. In one of his many proverbs, he observed;

> *"He who has knowledge restrains and is careful with his words, And, a man of understanding and wisdom has a cool spirit (self-control, an even temper). Even a [callous, arrogant] fool, when he keeps SILENT, is considered wise; When he CLOSES HIS LIPS, he is regarded as sensible (prudent, discreet) and a man of understanding."*
>
> **(PROVERBS 17:27-28 Amplified Bible)**

Speech can be golden at times and sometimes just a shade of yellow – but silence will always be golden. From the above scripture, it is clear that even a fool can be thought to be wise if he only keeps his mouth shut. You do not always have to talk. Sometimes, just bridle your tongue and let the moment pass. The 16th President of the United States of America, Abraham Lincoln made the following statement;

> *'It is better to remain silent and be thought a fool than to speak out and remove all doubt'*

Sometimes, we speak a lot intending to appear to be wise but then only appear foolish in the end. I like the word 'REMAIN' in Lincoln's statement. It suggests that there may be a tendency to react, to say something, to clap back, to respond, to correct something or someone. But if someone or something REMAINS in a particular state or condition, they stay in that state or condition and do not change.

Someone is reading this right now in the middle of a challenge, an argument, or a misrepresentation. You have a lot to say, and as a matter of fact, you seem to have some proof too, but silence is often a better defense than speech. Remember what Jesus did when they started hurling accusations and counter-accusations at him? He kept silent. Like a lamb being led to the slaughter. He kept silent.

As hard as it might be, it will do you a lot of good to learn to keep silent. The tongue is a small body organ but it is extremely powerful. It can hurt and it can build. It can lead to sin and it can lead to righteousness. It can break down and it can build up. So, before you put your mouth into gear; pause and confirm if your brain is engaged. The worst part is that once the words escape your mouth, you cannot swallow them back. The damage will already have been done. So, take your time and weigh every word. Pick your words with a toothpick and make sure your speech is always seasoned with salt – or better still, just keep quiet. Results have a way of speaking loudly!

1.7.1   Think and Act

a) What would you do to those who speak or go against you?
b) Think of the last time you spoke in anger – how did that affect you and your relationships?
c) Have you ever remained silent when being accused of something you didn't do?
d) Why do you think Jesus chose to remain silent when he was being wrongfully accused?
e) Think of things that you feel like responding to, can you see yourself refraining from responding?
f) How does that make you feel?

Personal Development

NOTES

Silence

NOTES

1.8 Day 8: Privacy Settings

My Transformational Thought today is:
'PRIVACY SETTINGS'

Privacy settings are controls available on much social networking and other websites that allow users to limit who can access your profile and what information visitors can see. Through the privacy settings section on your account, you can make your page/posts public, private, or limited to specific groups of people.

If you are on social media, it is important to meticulously check your privacy settings concerning the kind of content you share. But even before you change the settings, start by determining why you are on the social media network in the first place. Do you use the account for business? Or is it more of a social thing?

Privacy Settings

Do you use it for both business and social reasons? Understanding the why will help you know the best privacy settings for your accounts.

If you set the privacy settings to restrict anyone except you from accessing your posts, no one will ever see it and you might not get any interactions from friends and connections. On the flip side, if you set your posts to be visible to the general public, you might expose yourself to all manner of negative feedback and even cases of cyberbullying. Before you share any content on public social media accounts, you must first develop a tough skin. You must be ready to take in criticism and negative feedback without letting it get to you.

Social media is good when used responsibly. It increases your reach and it also makes it easier for others to reach you. Nowadays, headhunters use social media networks to look for talent. So, it is not just about hanging out with friends. Social media profiles can be used as an online CV as well.

Using social media responsibly means never posting content that you would be embarrassed of. You just never know when the HR manager will decide to check what you post on your social media accounts. Or worse still, you never know when a cyberbully will take advantage of something you shared and use it against you. Whenever you go on social media, always think of the Miranda warning, "anything you say or do can be used against you." So be responsible for what you say or do on social media. And use those privacy settings to ensure your posts are only seen by the intended audience.

It might help to do an honest social media audit. Is it helping you? Would you be better off without it? Maybe you want to trim down on the time you spend on social media? Or maybe you want to close down some social media accounts completely? Do not let social media ruin your life. Remember, social media is just a tool. Let it be your servant and never your master.

1.8.1 Think and Act

a) What's your end game with regards to social media?

b) Why are you on social media? (Why you're on a social networking site will determine what INFORMATION you share)

c) What are you benefiting from social media?

d) Are you being affected negatively by reactions you get from social networking sites?

NOTES

_____
_____
_____
_____
_____
_____

Privacy Settings

NOTES

Personal Development

NOTES

1.9 Day 9: Leverage

My Transformational Thought today is:
'LEVERAGE'

Some definitions of Leverage in the context of our thought for today are:

a) To use (a QUALITY or ADVANTAGE) to obtain a DESIRED effect or result

b) To use something that you already have, such as a resource, to achieve something new or better:

c) To use money to get the money

The desire to do a thing is an indication and proof that you have within you the power to do it. A wise man once said, "Every success opens the way for other successes." And also, "Desire is a manifestation of power." We all have lots of desires but if you want to be effective, you must zero down on the one thing you have the greatest desire for.

One premise state that an individual can do everything, but another premise takes it a bit further to state that, though the individual can do everything, they must not do everything. We must focus on the thing or things for which we have a stronger desire for, and do them to the best of our ability.

I have learned from other successful people and by personal experience that the reason many fails is not because of their lack of good ideas, creativity, or even desire, but because of inconsistency and a lack of dedication. Most failures in life happened because the individuals involved tried to do everything at every time and could not accomplish ANYTHING at ANYTIME. The problem with trying to be a jack of all trades is you will end up as a master of none.

Once you start focusing on one thing, you can then start leveraging on your successes to attain even greater successes. As I have already pointed out, every success opens the door for other successes. It is time you started to leverage your successes in one area to create successes in other areas.

1.9.1 Some practical examples

When Facebook started, there was no video call, they didn't have business promoting functionality, they didn't have Instagram to interface with, and there was also no Facebook Live. But they had success in their core function, which was connecting people and they then leveraged that function to create success in other areas. They had setbacks and challenges along the way too, but they used those challenges as opportunities to be better, do better, and become more successful.

Let's say you go to a flower garden and buy the seed of 10 types of flowers to plant like Orchids, Roses, Chrysanthemums, Tulips,

Leverage

Lilies, Poinsettias, Narcissus, Daffodils, Carnations, and violets. These flowers are all beautiful, some with a lovely fragrance, and some very popular because of their unique characteristics or cultural traits of their region.

If you plant them and do not give them the time and proper nurturing, though they have the potential to blossom, be beautiful and smell wonderful, they may not blossom to that stage, because there was no investment of the relevant time needed for them to come to their full potential. That doesn't mean you're a bad gardener. It could just mean that you can't care for 10 at the same time.

This flower analogy can also be translated into sports, relationships, businesses, investments, careers, hobbies, etc. If you try to cultivate 10 different things at the same time, you will be spreading yourself thin and that is a sure recipe for failure. But if you just picked on one thing and become good at it, you can then build upon that success by adding something else and before you know it, you will be excelling at lots of other things. That is the power of leverage.

1.9.2   Think and Act

a) List out all the things you are actively involved in presently.

b) What one, two, or three of those things are you focusing on? (Write them down)

Personal Development

c) Of the things you have written down, what do you have CAPACITY for? How much can you do at a given time/period? (Write it down)

d) What area/areas have you identified the most success in? (Write it down)

e) Do you have the ability to multitask? Can you do many things SUCCESSFULLY at the same time? Do you have facts to prove this? (State the facts)

NOTES

_____
_____
_____
_____
_____
_____
_____
_____
_____
_____
_____
_____
_____

NOTES

NOTES

PERSONAL EFFECTIVENESS

Personal effectiveness means harnessing all resources at your disposal to help you achieve your life goals. Everyone is unique and we all have different talents, strengths, skills, experiences, time, and energy- all these can be utilized to achieve personal effectiveness. Personal effectiveness requires effort and it cannot be achieved accidentally. You've got to take some deliberate action to see personal growth. Everything you do towards bettering yourself adds value to your life which ultimately contributes to your effectiveness. In this section, we will study some important skills that can help you to achieve your personal goals or grow your brand.

2.1 Day 10: Vision

My Transformational Thought today is:
'VISION'

Helen Keller (1880-1968) was the first deaf and blind person in history to earn a Bachelor of Arts degree. She then became a renowned author, political activist, and lecturer in the United States. One day, a journalist asked her what was worse than being blind. Her answer was,

> "the only thing worse than being blind is having sight but no vision"

What a profound truth! See, vision is more than sight – vision is the ability to see the invisible and comprehend the incomprehensible. It is the ability to go into the future while you are still in the present. Vision is what makes life worth living.

A story is told of two people (let's call them Jack and Tom) that were in the same predicament – they faced a similar problem under the very same environment. The two were presented with an idea with the potential of solving their problem.

Tom was immediately concerned about the financial implications of the idea. He was fully aware of how constrained he was financially and he allowed that to limit him. It's like the idea amplified his problems and it left him in a worse state of mind than he was before.

Meanwhile, Jack embraced the opportunity and looked beyond his financial constraints. He used the little resources he had to invest in the idea. Instead of looking at the problems the opportunity presented, he looked at the opportunities the problem presented. He took action and before long, he was able to turn his life the right side up. Jack possessed a positive mental attitude which influences him to look at the negative positively.

The difference between the two men was one had vision and the other didn't. Vision makes you optimistic about life because you are always excited about the prospect of a better tomorrow. From the bible, we read,

> *Where there is no vision, the people perish: Proverbs 29:18a*

The man that had no vision perished while his friend got out of the bad situation because he was a visionary. Life will always throw challenge after challenge in your direction and if you are visionary, you will always sail through.

Vision will remind you to keep your gaze on the goal. Vision will remind you to remain steady and focused on your aspirations. Vision will remind you not to allow interesting things to take your attention from the important. And when all is said and done, vision will help you to realize your goals in life.

2.2.1   Think and Act

a) Whenever you find yourself between a rock and a hard place, how do you respond? Are you a Jack or Tom?

b) Do you have the ability to identify opportunities in the face of adversity? If not,

c) How many challenges have you passed by because your mind was not open to see them for what they are - OPPORTUNITIES?

d) For the folks who attend church, many are in front of their great opportunity but still crying to God for financial breakthrough. You should start praying to God with these simple words, 'OPEN MY EYES OH LORD, TO IDENTIFY and MAXIMISE AMAZING OPPORTUNITIES'

Vision

NOTES

NOTES

2.2 Day 11: Planning

**My Transformational Thought today:
'PLANNING'**

Planning is the process of DECIDING in DETAIL how to do something before you start working on it. Everything in life rises or falls on planning. Poor planning results in definite failure and proper planning yields definite success. There is no such thing as accidental success. Every successful person invested lots of time in planning. Success is deliberate.

President Abraham Lincoln once said that if he was given 6 hours to fell a tree, he would spend the first 4 hours sharpening his axe. As excited as it may be to pursue your dreams, it pays to settle down and carefully lay down your strategy first. History is full of large armies that were defeated by small, less equipped, and supposedly inferior armies. One of the main reasons victory was achieved by the inferior army is they took time to develop a watertight battle plan.

Every CEO understands the value of developing a strategic plan for their company. In some cases, these plans span over decades but they still go ahead to make some short-term plans to guide their day to day operations. The same can be said of every successful country – they attained their heights of success through some diligent planning. Similarly, do not attempt to pursue anything before you create an action plan.

Planning is what separates successful ventures from unsuccessful ones. That is why the scripture says that God has a plan for your life.

> *"For I know the plans I have for you, declares the Lord, plans to prosper you and not to harm you, plans to give you hope and a future." Jeremiah 29:11*

God is a master planner. As Albert Einstein once said, *God doesn't play dice with the universe*. But it is not enough to know that he has a plan for your life – you should also follow suit and make a plan for your life as well. Granted, some people are naturally good at planning than others. But even if you are not a natural, planning is a skill that can be acquired through persistent practice. It might be difficult as you start out but after a while, you might find planning easy and even enjoyable.

Here are some practical steps that can help you to become better at planning.

Planning

1. Write down your goals. Research shows that you can increase the chances of meeting your goals by 42% just by writing them down. Picture what you want to achieve and once you have a clear mental image, put it down on paper.
2. Size down your plan. For instance, after you have developed your goals for the year, break the goals down into sizeable chunks. Instead of just leaving the goal as something you want to achieve in 12 months, identify the incremental steps you can take each week and each month to help you achieve that goal
3. Stay on target. The bigger your goals, the more focused you need to be. As you start knocking off milestones from the sized down plan, keep reevaluating your progress to make sure you are still on track.

2.2.1 Think and Act

a) Do you have an action plan for your life? And have you broken down the plan into bite-sizes?
b) What is your plan for today? What are you seeking to accomplish?
c) If you haven't done so already, make sure you write down your long-term and short-term plans. Remember, a goal written down is a goal half-achieved.

Like I often say, if it is not written, it's not real!

Remember, if you fail to plan, you have planned to fail and will fit into another person's MASTER-PLAN!

NOTES

Planning

NOTES

2.3 Day 12: Break Records

My Transformational Thought today is:
'BREAK RECORDS'

The dictionary defines 'Break Record' as to perform better, bigger, longer, etc., than anything else before.

In 1955, Guinness came with a clever marketing idea- they published a book of world records and distributed 50,000 copies of the book in different pubs in England. More than half a century later, most of the original world record entries have already been broken and new ones have been set. Official records show that the Guinness book of world records has at least 40,000 world records that have been set by people from all over the world.

You're not on this earth simply to break even. You are here to break rules, break RECORDS, and break THROUGH. You do not necessarily need to set a new world record or break an existing world record but you can still break records in your way. Just today, I beat a personal record in the gym on several exercises. You do not have to be preoccupied with their record or our record – just focus on your record. In the words of Lethia Owens,

> *"The goal in life is not to surpass the competition but to surpass the expectations we set for ourselves. Success is sweetest when we break our record, then wake up the next day ready to do it all over again."*

If you turn life into a competition, you will often get disillusioned and disappointed. You don't know why other people are running the race. You don't know their motivation or their goals – the only person you should be competing against is yourself. Strive to become a better version of yourself every day. If you achieved something significant last month, do not rest on your laurels. Instead, push yourself to become even better.

Apostle Paul is arguably the most successful Apostle in the Bible. But he didn't allow his success to get into his head. He knew he could always get better. He knew he could break his records. That is why he said,

> *Friends, don't get me wrong: By no means do I count myself an expert in all of this, but I've got my eye on the goal, where God is beckoning us onward—to Jesus. I'm off and running, and I'm not turning back. Philippians 3:13-14, MSG*

That should always be your goal – to keep pressing on towards a higher goal. And after achieving a goal, reset the goalposts. Do not let complacency to set it. do not allow yourself to stagnate. Don't count yourself an expert who needs no improvement – you must continually evolve to become better. Look at yourself in the mirror and remind yourself that you can do better today than you did yesterday.

2.3.1 Think and Act

a) What record are you pushing to break?

b) Who are you in competition with?

c) What goal have you set to achieve?

d) What ways are you planning to out-do yourself today, this week, this month, or this year?

e) How can you improve yourself to become a better version of yourself?

f) How can you come up with new ideas in improving yourself?

g) How are you planning to reinvent yourself?

NOTES

NOTES

2.4　Day 13: Do

My Transformational Thought today is:
'DO'

The word 'DO' can simply be defined as:

- to perform (an act, duty, role, etc.):
- to execute (a piece or amount of work):
- to accomplish; finish; complete:
- To take action

We often hear people say, "God said...", "God will do...", "God will give you..." As good as that may sound, what we need to hear more statements like, "I will do...", "I must do...", "I am going to...", etc.

You see, God has said many things and he will continue to speak – but after he speaks, you've got to do. You can't take a Laissez-faire attitude and assume that nature will just take its course. You have to do your part. Whoever said good things come to those who wait should have said that good things come to those who do – because it's true. The more you do, the more you get.

The writer of the book of Acts illustrated this in the opening sentence of the book;

> *In my first book, I told you, Theophilus, about everything Jesus began to DO and teach, Acts 1:1*

I must not fail to sound this warning, especially in this generation; Please try to stop yourself from teaching until you can DO.

Notice his reference to how Jesus operated – he began to DO and then to teach. This is one of many reasons why Jesus went down into history as the greatest teacher/preacher that ever-walked on earth. Unlike most teachers who preach water and drink wine, Jesus was a doer of everything he believed and taught.

You can borrow a leaf from the example of Christ. Do not live your life hoping things will somehow work out without having to lift a finger. Do not waste your years away as you wait for a miraculous break that will somehow fall into your lap. There is no such thing as an overnight success. most of the people that the media has branded an overnight success achieved the heights of success through hard work, determination, and self-sacrifice. While the rest of the world was asleep, they were steadily and unnoticeably working their way to the top, and when the world woke up, they had arrived at the zenith. Every successful person is a doer.

The reason why most people are still not realizing the kind of success they have always dreamt of is not that God is saying nothing. On the contrary, God has already said all they needed to hear about their life. The missing link is the doing part. As long as you are not doing, your life will not change.

I am reminded of the story of three lepers who were almost dying of hunger. They were camping outside the city because they were considered outcasts. The city was besieged by the army of an enemy so they had nothing much they could do. they were literally between a rock and a hard place. But then one day, they decided to do something about it. They figured if they remained in their comfort zone, they would die of hunger anyway. The only hope was to approach the enemy. There was a very big chance they would be killed on site but there was also a very small chance they would be welcomed and given some food.

> *Now there were four men with leprosy at the entrance of the city gate. They said to each other, Why stay here until we die? (2 Kings 7:3, NIV).*

So, they decided to go to the enemy's camp. As soon as they started walking, God amplified their steps and the enemy was terrified thinking a mighty army had ambushed them. To cut the long story short, the city that was on the verge of defeat was saved by 3 lepers who decided to DO rather than just seat and wait for fate.

My question then is, what if some individuals or organizations can amplify what you consider a very insignificant move?

And what if that provision is just sitting waiting for you while you are sitting waiting for a chance?

As you read this, you could be struggling in a certain area in your life. You might be struggling to make ends meet, struggling to maintain a relationship, struggling to fit in a new organization that doesn't value you, etc. whatever struggles you are dealing with, it is important to know that you already have enough ideas to change your life for the better. You probably have already identified what you need to do and who you need to meet. You have already worked out your detailed action steps. but now what you lack is the gusto to DO.

Don't think too long about it – just muster up the courage and start to DO!

2.4.1 Think and Act

a) Can you think of just one thing that can change if you decide to take action today? (Write it down)

b) Describe the feeling you will have if you decide to act on one creative idea in your mind? (Write it down)

c) What would you DO if you know there's no possibility of failure? (Write it down)

- So, what would you DO TODAY to PRODUCE wealth?
- Emphasis is not on the wealth but 'Do' and PRODUCE.
- And remember wealth in this context is not limited to finances.

d) What deliberate, calculated, and strategic steps are you willing to take TODAY that will bring you closer to reaching your goal?

e) What sacrifices are you willing to make? Sacrifices may include paying for a coach to train you, paying to take a course, stepping out of your comfort zone, walking away from unproductive associations and activities, etc.

NOTES

NOTES

Do

NOTES

2.5 Day 14: Problem-solving

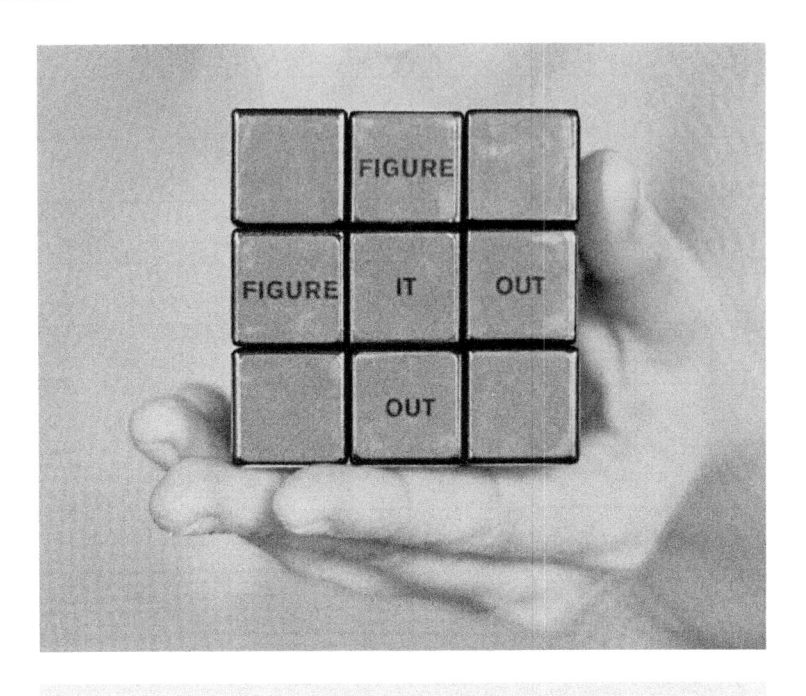

My Transformational Thought today is:
'PROBLEM-SOLVING'

Problem Solving is the process of finding solutions to difficult or complex issues.

We cannot run away from problems – if you attempt to, you will be running for the rest of your life because problems are part and parcel of life. But problems are good because they present unique opportunities. All the wealth of the world can be traced to problem solving.

See, if you solve a problem, people will be more than willing to pay you for the solution.

In the words of Earl Nightingale,

> *"The amount of money we receive will always be in direct ratio to the demand for what we do; our ability to do it; and the difficulty in replacing us."*

There was a shoe company that sent two salesmen to go scout out a remote village to see if there was a market for their shoes. On arrival, the salesmen were pleasantly surprised to find out that not a single soul in the entire village wore shoes. The first salesman went back to headquarters with the sad news. He said, "That's a bad market for us. They do not wear shoes in that village." But the second salesman came back with a different opinion. He said, "send me back with all the shoes you can get me! No one has shoes in that village!" The first salesman saw a problem and took off, the second one saw a problem and also saw a solution to the problem.

Every problem is an opportunity in disguise. And every problem is solvable. One of the significant skills in solving any problem is creativity. But creativity is not necessarily complex – you can still find creative and simple solutions. There is always a simple solution to every complex problem you encounter. All it takes is some creative thinking. Before you think about the solution, take time to think about the problem. Albert Einstein once said,

> *"If I had an hour to solve a problem, I'd spend 55 minutes thinking about the problem and 5 minutes thinking about solutions."*

Lateral thinking is one of the most effective problem-solving skills. It entails solving problems using an indirect and creative approach via reasoning that is not immediately obvious. It involves ideas that may not be obtainable using only traditional step-by-step logic. Effective problem solving will steer you away from a hammer even when it is the only tool available for a problem that does not involve nails.

As long as you start seeing problems as opportunities, you will always get a solution for them. Here are some tested problem-solving steps that can guide you in the process.

- Step 1. Identifying the problem - (understanding the WHAT)
- Step 2. Identifying the cause of the problem - (Understanding the WHY)
- Step 3. Identify and list out the possible solutions - (Brainstorming alone or with strategic stakeholders)
- Step 4. Generating and Evaluating likely Solutions - (Considering options and alternatives)
- Step 5. Decide on a solution
- Step 6. Implement the chosen solution
- Step 7. Evaluation, Contingencies, and Monitoring

2.5.1 Think and Act

a) Think of a recent problem that you encountered at the office/home. How did you respond to it? did you think of it as a problem or as an opportunity?

Problem-solving

b) Analyze the problem you identified above and identify the "Why" and the "What"

c) What are some of the opportunities that you should have seen in the problem that you didn't see?

d) What changes can you make today to ensure you become a better problem solver in the future?

NOTES

NOTES

NOTES

2.6   Day 15: Intentional

My Transformational Thought today is:
'INTENTIONAL'

Something intentional is deliberate or purposeful. **To be INTENTIONAL means** you are purposeful in word and action. It involves planning and strategizing.

It **means** you live a life that is meaningful and fulfilling to you. It **means** you make thoughtful choices in your life. **Being intentional means,** you actively interact and engage with your life.

Today is tagged 'Intentional Transformation'. This is a day to intentionally Initiate and establish a change in form, appearance, nature, or character. But as a warning, while you begin to do this, you may face strong opposition, especially from those who think they know you, those who think they know what you should do, those who think they know what you deserve, those who will accuse you of not joining the Joneses, buddying up with the bullies and running with the ruthless.

But that's okay.

You must understand that for most of us, our TRANSFORMATION will demand that we leave some folk behind, just as we leave some things behind. Before Abraham's transformation was realized, God asked him to leave his father's house and his country. Check it out;

> "The LORD had said to Abram, "Go from your country, your people and your father's household to the land I will show you.² "I will make you into a great nation, and I will bless you; I will make your name great, and you will be a blessing: **Genesis 12:1-2**

If Abraham hadn't obeyed the instruction to leave some folk behind, he would have never been made great. So do not worry too much about the connections that you have to lose along the way. it is all for the better. Great transformation requires great sacrifice.

Your TRANSFORMATION has to be INTENTIONAL because there will come that point where you will be pressured and tempted to RELAPSE into mediocrity, complacency, stinking thinking, sluggishness, poverty mentality, looser mindset, bullying, and even intimidation, etc. But that is when you have to stand your ground and say a firm 'NO'.

I can assure you of this one thing; if your TRANSFORMATION is INTENTIONAL, nothing thrown at you can BREAK You. On the contrary, you will always BREAK-THROUGH.

The first step in achieving a transformed life is achieving a REnewed mind. Your mind is more powerful than you give it credit for. There is so much damage that you can do to yourself just by harboring negative thoughts. Henry Ford famously said;

> *"Whether you think you can or can't, you are right."*

In simple terms, you are often a product of your thoughts. What you think of yourself will come to pass. You can't expect to be a huge success when all you think of is how you will be a failure. You cannot expect to be a winner in life when all you think of is how you are a big looser. Change your thoughts and you will change your life. Have a renewed mind and you will have a transformed life.

2.6.1 Think and Act

a) What are you intentional about today?

b) What have you set your mind to accomplish today? Have you planned to get it done?

c) What calculated steps do you INTEND to take towards achieving your goals today?

d) Are there any friends/acquittances that you need to let go to achieve your transformation?

Intentional

NOTES

Personal Effectiveness

NOTES

2.7 Day 16: Questions

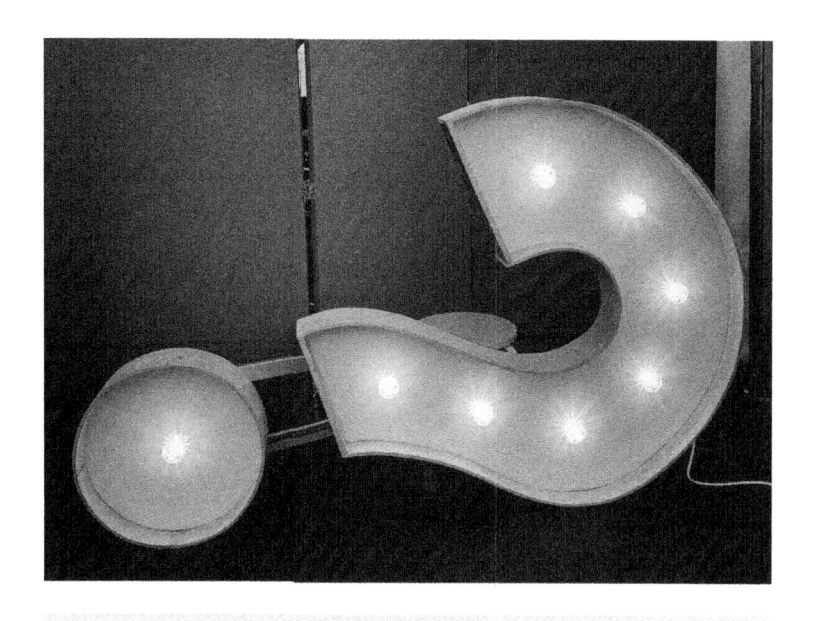

My Transformational Thought today is:
'QUESTIONS'

A QUESTION is a sentence that is worded or expressed to elicit information. It is a matter requiring resolution or discussion.

Every life coach will tell you that asking questions is one of the most important life skills. Questions are more important than answers. Even the right answer to a wrong question may not make a lot of difference. But the right question can be really powerful – even when there is no obvious answer. You should learn to ask yourself questions and you should be willing to respond to questions from your mentors and peers alike.

A question can take you down memory lane, it can take you into the future, or it can just inspire your creative juices to start following. Whenever you find yourself between a rock and hard place, just pose for a minute and ask yourself some questions like; "how did I get myself here?", "what are the possible solutions to my predicament?", "what can I do to avoid getting back here?", "whose help do I need to get out of this?"

Time spent on crafting the right questions is not time wasted. That is why when you visit your doctor, they don't rush to administer any medicine just based on their observation. They start by asking you some questions that will give them some history of your condition. In medicine, asking the right question is a matter of life and death – literally. And it's not just in medicine. Even in other facets of life, questions are very important.

Now, let me ask you some questions:

- What book have you read, reading, or studying this week or even this month? Including audiobooks. I'm not referring to your college books, work handbook, or the Bible.
- How are you developing your mind? And I'm not talking about reading posts from any social network site – yes, that includes my posts.

- What finite number of things are you telling your mind to work on? How have you challenged yourself mentally this week or even this month?

If you would be sincere to YOURSELF and write responses to all of these questions, you would have done a good assessment of your mind this week or this month. The responses to the above questions can help highlight what progress you are making in your personal development. If your responses are all negative, it means you haven't deliberately invested time in developing your mind.

But never too late for a fresh start. It's not too late to start today. They say the biggest room is the room for improvement. You can start by reading any of my books, they are a great read and very affordable too. 😁😄

Here are the titles:

i. Unlocking Supreme Intelligence - Activating Divine Intelligence and Discernment

ii. Generational Blessings - How to activate generational influence

iii. The Abundance of One - IDENTIFYING, DEVELOPING AND MAXIMISING THE ONE THING THAT HAS THE POTENTIAL TO TRANSFORM YOUR LIFE

I am also available to discuss and help you chart or plan a way to developing your mind, so, don't hesitate to reach out to me.

It's time to get KNOWLEDGE, READ because there is an entire world to LEAD.

2.7.1 Think and Act

a) Go back to the three questions I posed above and think critically about them and then write down the answers to the questions on a piece of paper.

b) Would you say you are putting some conscious effort into personal development? If yes, how can you improve? If not, what can you do to get started?

c) In what areas do you think you need most help? Feel free to reach out to me on this.

NOTES

NOTES

NOTES

2.8 Day 17: Insist

**My Transformational Thought today is:
'INSIST'**

I was reminded this morning that to receive certain things, we have to INSIST strongly within the confines of the contract, and in a biblical context, this means the word of God.

To INSIST means:

a) To be emphatic, firm, or resolute on some matter of desire, demand, intention

b) to dwell with earnestness or emphasis

If you insist that something should be done, you say it very firmly and refuse to take no for an answer. The word insist is only relevant when there's an absolute certainty of a specific goal. You can't insist on something you are uncertain about, or something you feel is right.

Insisting on something emboldens you to refuse any attractive alternative or substitute presented to you. It compels you to turn down a platter of attractive and highly-priced meals when all you want is fish and chips.

When it comes to being insistent, it by-passes what others think is good for you, suits you, or matches your need. it's rather what you KNOW you want.

It has to do with your knowledge and understanding of a particular thing, person, or even place that encourages you to be that resolute, and never back down. It empowers you to stand firm in the face of opposition, obstructions, and contradictions.

There is an interesting story in John 11 about the raising of Lazarus from the dead. Lazarus was not only dead but had been buried for 4 days. His body was already decomposing. But when Jesus appeared on the scene, he asked that they open the grave for him. Now, you must realize how bizarre that sounded. No one in his right mind would agree to such a request – but Jesus insisted. The Jews were not amused at this request. But because the sisters of the late Lazarus were good friends with Jesus, and because they believed in him, they agreed to the request. And the rest, as they say, is history.

Just like in the example above, sometimes you might need to make a request that may sound bizarre to some people. But once you are sure that it is the right thing to do, just insist on it. You might get on some people's nerves, you might lose some friends but as long as you put your foot down, you will still get what you want. As Thomas Jefferson said,

> *In matters of style, swim with the currents; but in matters of principle, stand like a rock.*

In other words, be firm when it comes to what you believe in. So, I guess the question is, what is it you are after that will compel you to be that resolute? Could it be that you have lost loads of opportunities, people, and things because you didn't know much about them?

Could it be that you have lost people and things as a result of your lack of being insistent because you gave up and walked away instead of demanding strongly?

2.8.1 Think and Act

a) Would you say that you insist on your goals? Or are you easily talked out of what you need to do?

b) What changes can you make to be firmer about your convictions?

c) Are there any opportunities that you have lost because you were not firm enough? What can you do to avoid that happening again?

NOTES

_____
_____
_____
_____

NOTES

Insist

NOTES

NOTES

3

FORGING AHEAD

It is said that winners never quit and quitters never win. How true and profound! If you persist on something, it will eventually work. Even a very hard rock can eventually be wearied off by a drop of water that keeps falling on it for years. Persistence will always pay off. One of the reasons why most people fail to achieve their goals is they often quit too soon. But if you can develop a mindset of always forging head, you will start to see great success.

Forging ahead, especially amid adversity, takes a unique kind of mindset. You have to look at things beyond the surface and you must be visionary. You must have an optimistic outlook that looks at setbacks as springboards. And that is what this section is all about – I will share some transformational thoughts that will put you in the right mindset to help you forge ahead.

3.1   Day 18: Obstacles

**My Transformational Thought today:
'OBSTACLES''**

An obstacle can be defined as:

a) something, material or nonmaterial, that stands in the way of literal or figurative progress:

b) something that obstructs or hinders progress

c) something that impedes progress or achievement

d) something that blocks you so that movement, going forward, or action is prevented or made more difficult

e) an object that makes it difficult for you to go where you want to go because it is in your way.

Someone once said, "Everything that is valued in life is guarded by OBSTACLES, and you have to overcome the OBSTACLES before you can take the valuable."

The fact that you see obstacles on your path should never deter you from your goals. If you look at the definitions above, it will become clear that obstacles are only in the way of someone that has a definite goal in life. Obstacles are therefore a confirmation that you are doing something right.

Obstacles can be the launching pad to propel you towards your goals. For an individual or organization that is DETERMINED, Obstacles do not block their path, they become the path. They become a test kit used in determining if what you desire is worth fighting for. Obstacles present a unique opportunity to pause and evaluate their goal, to see if it is worth the time and resources. When you face obstacles, you have the chance to make very definite decisions, tweak what needs tweaking, drop what, and who needs dropping and keep on keeping on.

An obstacle can only become gigantic when our goal is significantly reduced in our MINDS. If we continue to amplify our goals mentally, the obstacles will diminish, not necessarily in their literal size, but rather in comparison to our ability to handle them. Obstacles tend to force you to change your WHY or your decision to engage in the first place. But you must stay determined, be willing to change some things, but NEVER change your MIND.

To wrap it up, consider what Jesus had to say concerning those who turn away from their goal (the pursuit of God's kingdom)

> *"Jesus responded, "Why do you keep looking backward to your past and have second thoughts about following me? When you turn back you are useless to God's kingdom realm." [Luke 9:62 TPT]*

This means, when you turn back from your goals, you make yourself useless and the goal becomes valueless. Those who value their goals will never allow any obstacle to taking their gaze from the main goal.

3.1.1 **Think and Act**

a) What would you say is your main goal in life?

b) Is the goal worth the fight?

c) How determined are you to achieve your goal?

d) List some of the obstacles you have faced on the journey. How are you handling them? List down some action steps that can help you to surmount the obstacles.

NOTES

NOTES

NOTES

3.2 Day 19: Through

**My Transformational thought for today is:
'THROUGH'**

An intelligent writer once said, "The only way out is THROUGH." Whenever the going gets tough, quitting can look very appealing. But you should always remember that the only way out of the situation is to go right through it. sometimes, you get delivered from situations but most of the time, you will get delivered through the situations.

David in his assertion in the third verse of the twenty-third chapter wrote:

> 'Even though I walk THROUGH the darkest valley, I will fear no evil, for you are with me; your rod and your staff, they comfort me.'

So often we tend to want to run out, walk around, turn back from all the challenges in front of us. We want to shout or pray ourselves out. We ask God to take it away several times just like Jesus did in Gethsemane, but God says, you have to go THROUGH.

If you go through a particular experience or event, you experience it; and if you behave in a particular way through it, you behave in that way while it is happening.

The dictionary defines the word THROUGH as;

> *"IN at one end, side, or surface and OUT at the other:"*

2 things that happen when you go THROUGH a situation that involves God.

- IN
- OUT

It doesn't matter how bad that situation seems,

It doesn't matter how challenging it appears

It doesn't matter how sad the season becomes

It doesn't matter how many bids you lost

It doesn't matter the size of the opposition against you

It doesn't matter how they say your political career is in flames

It doesn't matter how many times you got fired

It doesn't matter how red your bank balance is,

If you are IN, then rest assured you will come OUT.

I believe this is the assurance that made the apostle Paul to write about getting excited in tribulation and trouble. Check it out;

Through

> *This doesn't mean, of course, that we have only a hope of future joys—we can be full of joy here and now even in our trials and troubles. Taken in the right spirit these very things will give us patient endurance; this in turn will develop a mature character, and a character of this sort produces a steady hope, a hope that will never disappoint us. Already we have some experience of the love of God flooding through our hearts by the Holy Spirit given to us. Romans 5:3-5, Philips*

Only those with a revelation can press on, keep walking and working, keep loving and caring, keep serving, and building in the face of trouble. What you make of your experience is reflective of what capacity you have. We read in the sixth verse of the eighty-fourth chapter of the psalms:

> *'As they pass THROUGH the Valley of Baka, they MAKE it a place of springs; the autumn rains also cover it with pools.*

It is human nature to try to find a way OUT of any contrary situation we find ourselves IN. But the question is, what way OUT do we choose? Do we go OUT from the same point we first got IN the situation - which means giving up or throwing in the towel, or do we go OUT on the other end of the process - coming out victorious, overcoming, conquering?

One thing you must remember is that at some point in your life you will go THROUGH but it totally up to you whether the experience will leave you better or bitter.

3.2.1　Think and act

a) Think of the last time you were between a rock and a hard place – would you say you went through it or did you call it quits?

b) Think of the last time you quit something because of too many obstacles on the path – what could you have done differently?

c) One of the reasons people fail to go through is the lack of a clear picture of where they are headed. Would you say your vision is clear? Have you developed S.M.A.R.T goals?

NOTES

NOTES

NOTES

3.3 Day 20: Fear

**My Transformational Thought today is:
What are you afraid of?**

This question can mean different things to different people. For some, FEAR stops them from DOING. For others, FEAR motivates them to DO. For those who don't DO, what is FEAR stopping you from DOING? For those who DO, what is FEAR motivating you to DO? Did you know that an ACTION motivated by FEAR can either be PRODUCTIVE or DESTRUCTIVE? So, which of these categories does your ACTIONS fall into?

The dictionary defines FEAR as:

> *"A THOUGHT that something unpleasant might happen or might have happened."*

But we also understand that THOUGHT becomes THINGS, because, an individual eventually BECOMES what they THINK. So, if it's just but a THOUGHT, why are you afraid?

Why do you spend all your thought and time preparing for something negative that may never happen instead of focusing all that creative thinking on something productive, something of substance that has the potential of changing your life and the lives of many?

FEAR can be crippling, not only because it can cause you not to DO, but because it can cause you to spend time on futility, pursuing shadows rather than investing time on substance.

>Your productivity becomes FUTILITY.

>You become exasperated for entirely NOTHING.

>You become ENRAGED rather than ENGAGED.

>You become INFURIATED rather than INFLUENCING.

Things and people you should be MANAGING start MADDENING you.

You start CONNIVING against those that have not CONTRIVED.

For someone living in England, FEAR can cause you to prepare for heatwaves in December, spending your resources on air conditioning rather than on heating. FEAR can motivate you into frying ice block hoping it remains crystallized.

You may have wasted so much time trying to fight an enemy that was never there in the first place, throwing punches in the shadows, launching missiles on an opposition camp that never existed. In the process, your worth, strength, value, and honour may have significantly disintegrated, and you may not even know it. It's time you woke because this is happening! It's FEAR - False Evidence Appearing Real.

Do not allow fear to cripple you. Always remember the words of President Franklin Roosevelt – the only thing to fear is fear itself. Begin to take steps toward your goals and aspirations with the determination and courage of a lion. And when you do so, all those irrational fears will start ebbing away until they are no more.

To sum it up, friends, I'd say you'll do best by FILLING your MINDS and MEDITATING on THINGS true, noble, reputable, authentic, compelling, gracious—the best, not the worst; the beautiful, not the ugly; THINGS to praise, not THINGS to curse.

[Philippians 4:8]

What are you AFRAID of?

3.3.1 Think and Act

a) What is your greatest fear when it comes to pursuing your life goals?

b) Does fear inspire you to positive action or cripple you?

c) What can you do to ensure fear doesn't stop you from achieving your goals?

d) List some of the things you didn't do in the past because of fear and list how many of those fears came to pass. Were you justified to be in fear?

NOTES

Fear

NOTES

3.4 Day 21: The Beautiful Pain

**My Tuesday Transformational Thought:
'The Beautiful PAIN'**

You must condition your mind to force your PAIN to PAY. Any pain that doesn't PAY you is a wasted opportunity. That's why I call it the Beautiful PAIN.

Pain can be very beneficial. When you step on a sharp object, pain tells you to quickly jump away. If you seat on a hot surface, pain tells you to jump off. Pain is nature's radar system. without pain, you would completely injure yourself without even knowing it. For instance, if you cut your finger by accident in the kitchen, you might not even notice it if the pain was non-existent. So, thank God for pain!

However, pain is not meant to stop you in the pursuit of your goals. On the contrary, it is meant to help you know how best to approach the journey. It is meant to tell you which pitfalls to avoid and what corrective mechanisms you need to employ. You can harness your pain for maximum benefit.

Pain should be a resource for development. It should be food for growth. This is not a problem shift - it's a Mindset shift because PAIN will and should happen, but you can choose to allow it to alter you or ADVANCE you.

Have a look at Joseph's analysis of his pain;

> *"You intended to harm me, but God intended it all for good. He brought me to this position so I could save the lives of many people." [Genesis 50:20, NLT].*

Joseph had a series of painful moments that seemed to happen in rapid succession. From his brothers plotting to kill him and eventually selling him as a slave to him being thrown into prison in a foreign land. It looked like all cards were stacked against him. But however bad the pain got; Joseph looked at the pain through the lenses of optimism. He knew something good would come out of all he was going through.

If you ever find yourself wondering why nothing you do seems to work, or where you have to deal with so much pain in your life, consider this – behind every great man/woman, there is always a great pain and a great shame. Your pain is directly proportional to your future. The greater your future, the more the pain. So do not despair because of the momentary pain that you have to endure.

Identifying, understanding, and maximizing your PAIN will not only liberate and advance you but will save MANY. So, the next time you experience pain, approach it with a different attitude. Look at the pain and say, "this PAIN's got to PAY."

Whenever you are doing anything worthwhile, there are always lots of excuses that can easily deter you from your path. But instead of listening to the excuses, you can choose to use them for your good.

- Use them to your advantage, to develop yourself.
- Use them to your advantage, to get knowledge
- Use them to your advantage, to make time, create time.
- Use them to your advantage to shadow someone, become an apprentice, learn something, and be teachable.

Do not allow the pain to be the excuse that excuses you from your dreams. On the contrary, use pain as radar and as a launching pad to chart a way forward.

Someday, maybe even today, you will get pain but instead of calling it pain, you will call it "The Beautiful PAIN"

3.4.1 Think and Act

a) Think about the pain that Joseph went through and ask yourself this – how did he come out of all that mess with such a positive outlook? What can you learn from his life?

The Beautiful Pain

b) Think of a recent pain you endured – would you say it left you better or it left you bitter? What are some lessons you can draw from your personal experience?

c) What is the way forward? How do you intend to deal with pain from now on?

NOTES

NOTES

NOTES

3.5 Day 22: Continue

My Transformational Thought today is:
'CONTINUE'

To continue means, to persist in an activity or process. To persist is to continue steadfastly or firmly in some state, purpose, course of action, or the like, especially despite of opposition, remonstrance, etc. The word 'CONTINUE' is only relevant for people who are ENGAGED in or COMMITTED to a particular activity, assignment, or goal.

My goal today is to encourage and challenge you to stay the course despite of difficulty or opposition. This is what Paul the entrepreneur and preacher said in 2 Timothy 4:7

> *"I have fought an EXCELLENT fight. I have finished my full course and I've kept my heart full of faith."*

If you look at that statement carefully, you will notice that everything Paul said was personal and individualized. He highlighted the fact that the only race or course you must, can and should finish is your course. Don't try to run other people's races. On the contrary, hyper-Focus on your own business. There is an African proverb that says,

> *'Don't take paracetamol for another person's headache'*

And another proverb puts it this way;

> *Take your nostril out of other people's business*

The only way to CONTINUE in what you are called to do is to ensure you do not get distracted by what other people are doing. Let each run their race and in the meantime, mind your own business. You must identify and stay your course without being distracted by the race of others. Another important truth to glean from the words of Apostle Paul is found in the statement, 'keeping your heart full of faith'

To keep your heart full of faith means to continue to believe in, trust, or support someone or something even when it is difficult to do so. The enemy knows how dangerous you are with a heart/mind full of faith, so he attacks you with doubt and unbelief. He knows that he does not have the authority to stop you, but he also knows that if he can get you mixed up in your mind or double-minded you will not receive anything.

An individual UNIFIED in their MIND regarding a particular thing, goal, or project is UNSTOPPABLE. Even God acknowledged this fact as we read in Genesis 11 verse 6, it states:

> *"The Lord said, "If as ONE people speaking the SAME language, they have begun to do this, then NOTHING they PLAN to do will be IMPOSSIBLE for them."*

So just focus on the one thing that you need to achieve and do not allow the interesting things around you to distract you from the important. Instead, continue doing what you started to do. It might not look like much in the beginning but if you stick to it, you will eventually have a lot to show for your efforts.

3.5.1 Think and Act

a) What is your course?

b) Have you identified your course as EXCELLENT or UNIQUE?

c) How hard are you FIGHTING?

d) How easily do you CAVE in?

e) Are you keeping your heart FULL of faith?

Continue

NOTES

NOTES

3.6 Day 23: Decisions

**My Transformational Thought today is:
'DECISIONS'**

The dictionary defines Decision as the act of, or need for making up one's mind.

A Decision is a conclusion or resolution reached after consideration.

In psychology, decision-making is regarded as the cognitive process resulting in the selection of a belief or a course of action among several alternative possibilities. Decision-making is the process of identifying and choosing alternatives based on the values, preferences, and beliefs of the decision-maker. Every decision-making process produces a final choice, which may or may not prompt action.

Joshua, while speaking to the people he was assigned to lead, presented them with choices that should prompt a decision.

In Joshua 24:14-15, we read;

> *"Now, therefore, fear the Lord and serve him in sincerity and in faithfulness. Put away the gods that your fathers served beyond the River and in Egypt, and serve the Lord.*
>
> *And if it is evil in your eyes to serve the Lord, choose this day whom you will serve, whether the gods your fathers served in the region beyond the River, or the gods of the Amorites in whose land you dwell. But as for me and my house, we will serve the Lord."*

The decision even as it applies to us this day has to be made between the gods and the Lord. God also put out a communication to the people in Deuteronomy 30:15-20, and He said:

> *[15] See, I set before YOU today LIFE and PROSPERITY, death and destruction.*
>
> *[16] For I command you TODAY to love the Lord your God, to walk in obedience to him, and to keep his commands, decrees and laws; then you will live and increase, and the Lord your God will bless you in the land you are entering to possess.*
>
> *[17] But if your heart turns away and you are not obedient, and if you are drawn away to bow down to other gods and worship them, 18 I declare to you this day that you will certainly be destroyed. You will not live long in the land you are crossing the Jordan to enter and possess.*

> *[19] This day I call the heavens and the earth as witnesses against you that I have set before you LIFE and death, BLESSINGS and curses. Now CHOOSE life, so that you and your children may live*
>
> *[20] and that you may love the Lord your God, listen to his voice, and hold fast to him. For the Lord is your life, and he will give you many years in the land he swore to give to your fathers, Abraham, Isaac and Jacob.*

We have a responsibility to decide between life and prosperity or death and destruction. This is a good point for us to realize that we must stop passing blame and take responsibility for where we are. It will interest you to know that your behavior, not your confession is a clear reflection of what you have chosen. That's because, words are displayed in confession, but expectations are characterized by behavior.

I want to pause at this point and remind you that every decision making has consequences, good or bad. Decision-making can be regarded as a problem-solving activity yielding a solution deemed to be optimal, or at least satisfactory. Having the intelligence of God in us but yet staying in a position of perplexity is like having a loaded bank card that is not activated, it can't buy you anything. Or, it's like starting a powerful automobile, but refusing to open the throttle, yet complaining there's no movement.

The throttle of a motor vehicle or aircraft is the device, lever, or pedal that controls the quantity of fuel entering the engine and is used to control the vehicle's speed. You must understand that in us we possess so much power that has not been put to use. We have the power to control our speed. People often say, be careful of a praying person. But I say, be careful of a praying person, who also possesses the ability to make sensible decisions QUICKLY.

3.6.1   Think and Act

a) How quickly do you usually make a decision when the occasion demands it?

b) What decisions will you make today in advancing your life?

c) What associated STEPS or ACTIONS will you take in implementing the decisions you have made today?

NOTES

_____
_____
_____
_____
_____
_____
_____
_____

Decisions

NOTES

NOTES

3.7 Day 24: Precision

My Transformational Thoughts this morning:
'PRECISION'

Precision is defined as the quality, condition, or act of being exact and accurate. Donald Rumsfeld, an American politician said;

> "Be Precise. A lack of PRECISION is dangerous when the margin of error is small'.

Yesterday while practicing golf, I discovered that proper planning and practice can increase PRECISION. I was able to hit 2 balls to land at the same spot in a row. In other words, I was able to get an exact 'Angle of Attack' back to back.

But this PRECISION only happened because I PLANNED and PRACTICED. See, precision cannot come by accident. It comes through deliberate effort and planning. It comes through diligence.

> *Seest thou a man diligent in his business? he shall stand before kings; he shall not stand before mean men. Proverbs 22:19*

As you become diligent in your business, you achieve precision and that precision will set you before kings. Tiger Woods is a great example of this. He was once asked how much time he spends practicing and he revealed that he typically spends close to 8 hours a day practicing. Can you imagine training for one tournament all year round for 8 hours a day? No wonder he is such a legend!

And just in case you are wondering – no, it is not just a golf thing. On the contrary, this is a life lesson that you can apply in almost any sphere of your life. If you take your time to plan then spend enough time in practice, you will easily rise to the top in your field of specialization.

Another great example of how diligence pays off is the invention of the light bulb. Reportedly, Thomas Edison had to try out 999 experiments before the thousandth one finally worked. Someone asked him if he felt like a failure after he failed over 900 times. He was shocked at the question and responded emphatically that he hadn't failed at all but on the contrary, he had discovered 999 methods of how not to make a light bulb. Can you imagine trying to do something and failing 999 times in a row? Not very many people would manage that – but it is this diligence that made Edison go down in history as the man who invented the light bulb.

And that's the thing with precision – it doesn't come automatically or on a silver platter. It comes on the altar of sacrifice, planning, and practice. Before a surgeon can operate on a patient, he has to spend hours practicing on a cadaver. Only after rigorous training and practice will they be allowed to use a scalpel on a real patient. Every surgeon knows precision is a matter of life and death. And that is the right attitude when pursuing your goals – always strive for precision.

3.7.1 Think and Act

a) Would you describe yourself as diligent? If yes, what makes you say so? If not, what changes do you need to make to be diligent?

b) Do you find yourself completing a project for the sake of meeting a deadline or do you fixate on giving it the best you've got?

c) Think of one time when you executed something with precision. How did that make you feel?

NOTES

NOTES

3.8 Day 25: Expectations

**My transformational thought for today is
'EXPECTATIONS'**

Your expectations are your strong hopes or beliefs that something will happen or that you will get something that you want. One of the leaders I have grown to respect once said;

> *"It's not that we aim too HIGH and miss, but rather that we aim too LOW and hit."*

Are your expectations based on other people's expectations of you? Are you living life from another person's script? Have you capped your expectations as a result of your background, family, or the small-minded, shallow thinking jokers you have surrounded yourself with? Here is the thing - one of the reasons most people get excited when you achieve something seemingly great, is because you just reached their expectations of you.

Your efforts will be futile if you expect people to push you to achieve something they don't seem to have the capacity to contain. You must learn to develop your expectations. Forget about what other people are expecting from you for a minute and just focus on your own expectations.

In most cases, what you receive in life is based on your expectations. The expectation has a kind of magnetic power that pulls whatever we are expecting. When you are expecting something, you are fully persuaded that it will happen. That is why the same word is used for expectant mothers. An expectant mother knows that after nine months, they will receive a baby. So, they make preparations for the baby in advance. Their motherhood instincts kick in and they start nesting long before the baby arrives. That is how expectation works.

In Ephesians 3:20, Paul reminds us of the power of expectation. He says,

> "Now to him who is able to do immeasurably more than all we ask or imagine, according to his power that is at work within us,"

From this scripture, God does more than just answering our prayers – he also does way above whatever we imagine or expect. So, you better start developing some positive expectations! Start by reminding yourself that you have more to offer than what other people expect. Remind yourself that there is more to you than meets the eye. And then go ahead and start expecting great things.

3.8.1   Think and Act

But before you feel good about your achievements, pause and think about it.

a) What if you are worth more?

b) What if you can do more?

c) What if YOU are more?

NOTES

NOTES

NOTES

3.9 Day 26: Concentration

**My Transformational Thought this morning:
'CONCENTRATION'**

Concentration is defined as 'an exclusive attention to one object; a close mental application.' It is the direction of attention to a single object. Concentration on something involves giving ALL your attention to it. The decision to apply oneself to one particular thing, focusing and concentrating on it has the power to change your lives.

I think our challenge most times is not that we get involved with so many things, but as Jesus put it, we are fussing far too much and getting ourselves worked up over them, and by doing that become futile in our effort - our productivity is minimized or hampered.

> *Luke 10:38-42 MSG*
>
> *"As they continued their travel, Jesus entered a village. A woman by the name of Martha welcomed him and made him feel quite at home. She had a sister, Mary, who sat before the Master, hanging on every word he said. But Martha was pulled away by all she had*

> *to do in the kitchen. Later, she stepped in, interrupting them. "Master, don't you care that my sister has abandoned the kitchen to me? Tell her to lend me a hand."*
>
> *The Master said, "Martha, dear Martha, you're fussing far too much and getting yourself worked up over nothing. One thing only is essential, and Mary has chosen it—it's the main course, and won't be taken from her."*

Martha thought the master wanted her to be very busy serving him. But Mary chose to ignore all the chores that needed to be done and concentrate on Jesus. After all, she didn't know if she would ever get such an opportunity again. The greatest prophet and teacher in Israel, the Messiah himself, was seated right there in their living room! This called for concentration! Meanwhile, Martha was getting worked up on how her sister was just sitting there instead of helping her.

There are lots of things in your life that are just treadmills – they keep you busy and occupied but they take you nowhere. It pays to slow down and decide what you want to concentrate on. When you start concentrating on what you are supposed to be doing, you will start noticing things that have escaped your attention for decades. You will suddenly notice the chirping bird on the tree and the butterfly in the garden. Life will get more beautiful, more rewarding, and more fulfilling.

Never mistake being busy for being productive. It is better to concentrate on one thing and have it done right than to try to do several things at the same time without achieving anything worth writing home about. This is why you must "minimize" your life and concentrate on what is important. Never feel bad about having to say no to some people or something. You are not meant to please everyone around you. Even if your sole purpose was to please everyone, you would never accomplish it. Even Jesus had his fair share of enemies. So just take the bull by the horns and concentrate.

3.9.1 Think and Act

a) What one thing (goal-related) in your life can you choose to focus on today?

b) You can start by finding a book that aligns with your goal and read it for an hour

NOTES

NOTES

Concentration

NOTES

NOTES

GO FOR IT!

Life is not and will never be fair. If life was fair, innocent people would never be subjected to suffering. If life was to be fair, there would be so many impoverished hard-working people. Because life is not fair, it will not give you what you deserve – but it will give you what you demand. That explains why some people are getting a raw deal while others are getting much more than they deserve. Those who demand the best out of life eventually get it.

If you want to rise to the top in your area of specialization, you must start demanding what you want in life. You must develop the kind of tenacity and faith that refuses to take a no for an answer. You must be willing to do the impossible, see the invisible and conceive the inconceivable. In this section, we will look at some transformational thoughts that can help you achieve this and more.

4.1 Day 27: Create

My transformational thought for today is:
'CREATE'

Some definitions of the word 'CREATE' are:

- to cause to come into being, as something unique that would not naturally evolve or that is not made by ORDINARY processes.
- to evolve from one's THOUGHT or imagination, as a work of art or an invention.

The word CREATE is a very powerful word that is not often pondered on because of the tasking responsibility of exercising or applying the mind.

It is different from 'MAKE' or 'MADE'. The difference between something being **created** and something being **made** is that when something is **created**, it is brought into existence out of **the invisible**. But when something is **made,** it is formed out of SOMETHING else that already exists.

Let's check these 2 Bible references with regards to the supreme CREATOR and MAKER, God:

Genesis 1:1-2:

> *In the beginning, God **CREATED** the heaven and the earth.*
>
> *And the earth was without form, and void; and darkness [was] upon the face of the deep. And the Spirit of God moved upon the face of the waters.*

Genesis 1:27:

> *And God **MADE** man in His own LIKENESS. In the likeness of God He made him. He made both male and female."*

God is both a creator and a maker. And remember, the man was made in his image and his likeness. He also put the ability to create and make in man. But the problem has never been the making. Man's history is full of lots of things that are made. From making a cup of coffee to manufacturing automobiles, man has excelled at making. But unfortunately, man is doing very poorly in creating.

The few who have engaged that power to CREATE seem to be the minority that controls the wealth in a nation. They employ the majority, get served by the majority, and in many ways applauded by the majority. They are the 5-10% who control the resources that govern and manage 90%-95%. While makers come up with stuff by combining existing products, creators come up with totally new inventions that one can argue were pulled out of the invisible.

Go for it!

Creating calls for a high level of creativity and imagination. Creators have to dare to believe that the impossible is possible. most things that are created seemed Ludacris before they were conceptualized. But the creators who came up with the ideas are now celebrated. To be a creator, you must be willing to swim against the currents, and only then will you realize your unique dreams.

4.1.1 Think and Act

a) What's stopping you from engaging your creativity? What's stopping you from chasing that dream?

b) What idea have you conceived but are afraid of exploring?

c) How about deciding to start today and right now?

NOTES

_____
_____
_____
_____
_____
_____
_____
_____
_____

Create

NOTES

Go for it!

NOTES

4.2 Day 28: No Middle Ground

My Thursday Transformational Thought:
'NO MIDDLE GROUND'

Being in the middle ground means doing nothing about anything. It means sitting on the fence while people on both sides of the fence are busy doing something about their dreams. You cannot afford to be in the middle ground if you want to achieve your dreams.

In the book of Revelation, God speaks a warning against the people who are sitting in the middle ground. Check it out;

> "I know you inside and out, and find little to my liking. You're not cold, you're not hot—far better to be either cold or hot! You're stale.

> *You're stagnant. You make me want to vomit." (Revelation 3:15-176 MSG)*

Be careful not to hang around people who are neither here nor there. People that do not stand for anything will also fall for anything. These are the kinds of people that were described in Revelation as 'STAGNANT and STALE.' They have lost freshness, vigor, quick intelligence, initiative, or the like. And they can be a really bad influence on you. It is better to hang around people who are leading a purpose-driven life – people who are actively pursuing their goals.

Do everything within your power to ensure you are not sitting on the fence. Here is the thing - you **are** either working very hard to succeed or you **are** working very hard to fail. There is no middle ground when it comes to success. It is important to note that nothing just happens. Everything you see happening all around you happens because someone is making it happen. Newton's first law of motion states,

> *"a body a body at rest will remain at rest unless an outside force acts on it, a body at rest will remain at rest unless an outside force acts on it, and a body in motion at a constant velocity will remain in motion in a straight line unless acted upon by an outside force.."*

Simply put, if you see something moving, it's because some external force has been applied on it by someone or something. If nothing is moving in your life, it means you stopped applying the required force. It means you are resting on your laurels. And until you break out of that status quo, nothing will change.

4.2.1 Think and Act

a) What are you working very hard to achieve?

b) Is there any area in your life where you have left everything to fate?

c) Do you find yourself hanging around a bunch of people who are headed nowhere?

d) What are some positive steps you can take to avoid sitting in the middle ground?

NOTES

Go for it!

NOTES

Create

NOTES

4.3 Day 29: Don't Quit

My Transformational Thought today is:
'DON'T QUIT

For particular emphasis, I will put the lens on the word 'QUIT.' The dictionary defines the word 'QUIT' as:

- to stop, cease, or discontinue:
- to give up or resign; let go; relinquish
- to stop trying, struggling, or the like; accept or acknowledge defeat.

I will make it clear from the very onset, quitting is a choice. It is not an accident nor something imposed on anyone. There may be circumstances that can cause someone to quit, but ultimately, the individual has to make a decision.

Quitting mostly happens when the pain or challenges in the process outweighs your initial purpose or benefit for engaging thereof. And this mostly happens in the mind. Suffice it for me to say that one of the most dangerous persons to embark on a journey or a project with is a person with a quitting mentality. These are the kinds of people who will have their hands on the job but their minds will always be miles away.

But What is the real reason for quitting? How do you establish the highest degree of pain you can handle? What parameters do you use in measuring the closeness to your goal in comparison to the pain that's prompting you to quit? I once heard a man say that he was leaving his job because the pain of keeping it outweighed the joy of staying home with his family. He wanted to call it quits. In his mind, he had reached the end of the road. He found everything negative about the job and used that as his standpoint to leave.

But while he was planning to hand in his resignation, his boss on that same day had prepared a promotion, salary increase, and more benefits for him. Needless to say, he kept back his letter, took the offer, and got excited. He created in his mind NEW positive thoughts about the organization which made him stay.

Could it be that the reconfiguration of your mind can enhance your staying ability? Could it be that CHOOSING to focus on at least one positive aspect of your journey can influence your decision not to QUIT? Perhaps you may have lost sight of the original purpose of the journey?

In closing consider this profound statement that was made by prophet Isaiah;

This statement from Isaiah is very profound:

> *"People with their minds set on you (God), you keep completely whole, steady on their feet, because they keep at it and don't quit." (Isaiah 26:3, MSG)*

4.3.1 Think and Act

Create

NOTES

Go for it!

NOTES

4.4 Day 30: Wise Counsel

**My Transformational Thought today is
'WISE COUNSEL'**

I have seen by experience the benefits of wise counsel. Wise counsel can mean the difference between success and failure. Do not choose your core advisers out of sentiments. If you must rest your head/mind, it must be on those who operate in the wisdom of the Lord.

> "For God promises to keep in perfect peace, those whose minds are placed on Him."- Isaiah 26:3

One thing I have always desired from God is to bless me not just with people, but people whose heads are functional, people of wisdom. An ignorant man surrounded by foolish counsel most likely will make foolish decisions. But an enlightened man surrounded with wise counsel is likely to make wise decisions.

Many kings, leaders, captains of industry, and intelligent people have been destroyed because of the people they surrounded themselves with.

> *"Plans succeed through good counsel; don't go to war without wise advice." [Proverbs 20:18 NLT]*

Ideas, businesses, wars, and even court cases with the potential to succeed have failed because of ignoring WISE COUNSEL.

> *"A wise man is strong, and a man of knowledge strengthens his power; For by wise guidance you can wage your war, and in an abundance of [WISE] counselors there is victory and safety." [PROVERBS 24:5-6 AMP]*

WISE COUNSEL is invaluable, and it is different from good advice. Wise Counsel will help you identify what is ultimately good and what is just currently popular. It will help you differentiate what is VALUABLE from what is just CHEAP. It will guide you not to make permanent decisions based on temporary challenges. With good advice, a couple can buy a house, but with WISE COUNSEL a couple can buy a house that will continue appreciating in its value.

In closing, you must be familiar with the saying; "a word is enough for the wise." This is one of my favorite sayings. It raises some questions which I want to suggest.

Create

Which word is enough for the wise?

- Whose word is enough for the wise?
- And finally, who are the wise?

4.4.1 Think and Act

a) Do a personal evaluation and check the core people around you, and ask yourself; "what do they bring to the table?"

b) Check the decisions you have made this week that involve people, what advice have you received, and what are the outcomes?

NOTES

_____
_____
_____
_____
_____
_____
_____
_____
_____

Go for it!

NOTES

Create

NOTES

4.5   Day 31: Personal Action

My Transformational thought today is:
'PERSONAL ACTION'

Action is doing something for a PARTICULAR purpose. It is the fact or process of doing something, TYPICALLY to achieve a goal. The failure to connect PERSONAL ACTION to thought or faith can lead to futility or merely wishful thinking. If you do not match your desire with some PERSONAL ACTION, you will only be building mansions in the sky so to speak.

Your bank account will not get filled up suddenly. Your garden will not look beautiful just from the blues. Your body will not look trimmed or muscular in the twinkling of an eye. You must

PREPARE for the things you have thought or prayed about through WORK.

As we come to the close of this study, it is important to note that unless you put the concepts shared in this material to work, the study will remain just that – a study. But if you want the transformational thoughts shared herein to transform your life, you must take action.

The Chinese have a saying that the best time to plant a tree was 20 years ago but the second-best time is now. The best time to take action was on day 1 of this series. The second-best time is now. Make up your mind to take some action steps towards your goals.

Dreaming is good but after the dream, wake up and chase the dream. If you remain in bed in the hope that you will dream some more, you will never really actualize any dream. I am speaking in the metaphorical sense of it. Only those who actively pursue their dreams will ever realize the fruition of those dreams. The rest will remain in the valley of wishful thinking.

Taking action doesn't have to be scary. The journey of a thousand miles begins with a single step. You don't have to take a huge leap of faith – just take some baby steps. Just continue putting one foot ahead of the other and before you know it, you will have covered a thousand miles. The more you procrastinate taking a step, the more other people are covering more ground. It's time you stopped procrastinating and started taking some visible steps towards your goals.

4.5.1 Think and Act

a) What are your deliberations today/this very moment? (List them)

b) What are you doing about it? (List plans)

c) What Personal Action would you take in preparation for their manifestation? (Write it down) – for example, register the business name, enquire about opening a business account, etc.

NOTES

NOTES

Go for it!

NOTES

4.6 Day 32: Goodbye

My transformational thought for today is
'GOODBYE'

A **goodbye** means that someone's departing. The original **goodbye**, dating from the 1570s, was godbwye, which was a contraction of the **farewell** phrase "God be with ye!"

I have used goodbye so many times and in so many ways, but the emphasis is always on GOOD. This means, you don't have to leave anyone because they are bad and done wrong, but when you juxtapose them with your goal, destiny, or assignment, they fall out of scope. So, you have to be bold, but loving and caring enough to say GOODBYE.

See, not everyone in your life is necessarily going the same direction as you. And that is not to mean that you are better than anyone else. You are often not. But it is best to understand that where you are headed might not necessarily be where everyone else is headed. And when you realize this, the best thing you can do is to say part ways and say goodbye.

Sometimes, you might be headed in the same direction with someone but after a while, a fork on the road comes up. This is usually the hardest of all goodbyes. Because you have traveled together for so long, it is often heartbreaking to say your goodbyes. The temptation is often to just follow them on the diversion they take. But do not fall to the temptation. Stick to your road and say your goodbyes. Maybe, just maybe, your paths will cross again but even if they don't, nothing will ever replace the joy and fulfillment of knowing you achieved your purpose by sticking to your path.

The pain of saying Goodbye might linger for a long time but it will come nothing close to the pain of regret - that of knowing that if you had said your goodbye when you had the chance, you would be better off today. Jesus understood this pretty well and that is why he never allowed his emotions to distract him from the goal. In as much as he loved hanging around people and meeting their needs, he knew the importance of saying goodbye when occasion demanded it. check this out;

> *"After telling everyone good-bye, he went up into the hills by himself to pray."*
>
> **Mark 6:46 NLT**

Goodbye

The burden of 'things' can greatly hinder our progress in life. Jesus left his company and activities behind and went UP the hills by himself. For the most part, GOING UP demands that you leave people behind. It might mean walking them to the car, hugging and kissing them, calling them, sending them a text, etc. but whatever it takes, learn to say GOODBYE.

4.6.1   Think and Act

a) When was the last time you said a "Goodbye?"

b) Do you find yourself hanging around people who are not adding any value to your life?

c) Take a piece of paper and write down some names of people that you need to say goodbye to and determine to do it sooner than later.

NOTES

_____
_____
_____
_____
_____
_____
_____

Go for it!

NOTES

Goodbye

NOTES

Go for it!

Printed in Great Britain
by Amazon